HMS WARRIOR 1860

CONTENTS

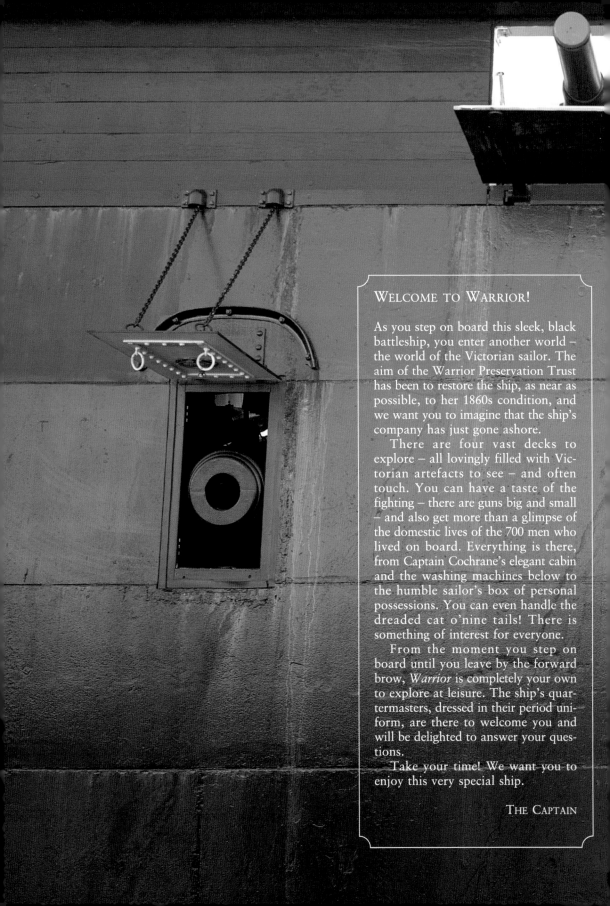

WELCOME TO WARRIOR!

As you step on board this sleek, black battleship, you enter another world – the world of the Victorian sailor. The aim of the Warrior Preservation Trust has been to restore the ship, as near as possible, to her 1860s condition, and we want you to imagine that the ship's company has just gone ashore.

There are four vast decks to explore – all lovingly filled with Victorian artefacts to see – and often touch. You can have a taste of the fighting – there are guns big and small – and also get more than a glimpse of the domestic lives of the 700 men who lived on board. Everything is there, from Captain Cochrane's elegant cabin and the washing machines below to the humble sailor's box of personal possessions. You can even handle the dreaded cat o'nine tails! There is something of interest for everyone.

From the moment you step on board until you leave by the forward brow, *Warrior* is completely your own to explore at leisure. The ship's quartermasters, dressed in their period uniform, are there to welcome you and will be delighted to answer your questions.

Take your time! We want you to enjoy this very special ship.

THE CAPTAIN

WARRIOR FACTS AND FIGURES

Ordered:	11 May 1859
Launched at Blackwall:	29 December 1860
First commissioned at Portsmouth:	1 August 1861
End of service as a first-line warship	15 September 1871
Commissioned as ship of First Reserve	1 April 1875
Ended active service:	31 May 1883
Commissioned as stationary depot ship	16 July 1902
Commissioned as Vernon III at Portsmouth:	December 1904
Paid off as part of HMS Vernon	31 March 1924
Arrived as fuelling hulk at Pembroke Dock:	16 March 1929
Handed over for restoration at Hartlepool:	12 August 1979
Returned to Portsmouth:	16 June 1987

The Navy of 1860 was very different from what it had been in Nelson's time. In the years between, our old enemies, the French, had avidly adopted any technological advance that might give them the upper hand. Every few years, despite its entrenched conservatism, the Admiralty was jolted into a response, and the service was forced through the biggest physical and social changes of its 1100-year history.

The first of these was the coming of steam. By 1840, the French were challenging Britain's hitherto undisputed naval might with small, manoeuvrable steam vessels mounting the latest in guns. Inevitably, French boasts and repeated rumours of invasion stung the Admiralty into building several large paddle frigates armed with a small number of very heavy guns. But paddles were vulnerable to attack, and took up the space of many guns.

These frigates were eclipsed at their zenith by the screw propeller, more powerful than the paddle and less restrictive on gun space. Developments came thick and fast, for with screw propulsion and new horizontally-driven engines safe below the waterline, even battleships could be steam propelled.

But advances in propulsion were matched by improvements in firepower, and better protection became urgently needed. In the past, wood-hulled ships had been more than a match for round shot – during Trafalgar not one English ship had been sunk – and victories were usually won by dismasting and boarding. But now the French had come up with explosive shells capable of destroying any ship within their admittedly limited range. These shells became standard in the French fleet in 1837, the British reluctantly following suit two years later. Stronger ships were needed, and experiments with iron vessels began. These were so unpromising – the iron shattered into lethal fragments – that tests were abandoned in 1851. It was the Crimean War that proved the turning point, shells from a Russian squadron wiping out the wooden Turkish fleet at Sinope. The French answer was to build long armoured gun barges with 4-inch (10cm) iron plate backed by thick wood. These proved instantly successful at Kinburn in 1855, but yet again the Admiralty proved stubborn, and battleship design remained unchanged – but not for long.

Meanwhile changes of great moment had occurred in naval organization. In

1830 officers who left the sea had stayed not just on half pay but on the promotion ladder as well. The result was that the Navy was run by men too old to cope in a time of rapid change; also the bright young men who were desperately needed at the top could not get there. Again, war in the Crimea cruelly exposed these weaknesses and the Admiralty was forced to act. By 1860 the blockage was clearing fast, a much higher proportion of paid officers being on active service.

Changing technology meant the need for specialized officers and with this came major changes in the social hierarchy of the ship. For centuries, the non-military jobs – purser, sailing master, chaplain, surgeon, etc. – had been performed by warrant officers. But as ships grew more complex, these tasks became more important, and commissioned officers were appointed to perform them. In the early days, an engineer was just a mechanic, sent aboard by the steam engine maker to wield his spanner and live amongst the sailors. Then in 1836 the Engineer Branch was formed, but even its senior officers ranked only with lesser warrant officers – carpenter, boatswain, etc. You will see, though, from *Warrior*'s wardroom that by 1860 the two chief engineers had achieved commissioned status – although only at a low level.

The need for a more professional approach to a variety of skills meant that formal training was introduced into the service. From the 1820s schoolmasters had begun to appear on ships and, after earlier attempts had failed, the Portsmouth-based HMS *Illustrious* (replaced soon by HMS *Britannia*) began training all new officer entrants.

Amongst the men too, there had been big changes in the way things were done. In Nelson's day, sailors were pressed into service, by force if necessary, and were paid off at the end of their ship's commission – if they hadn't deserted first! With advances in gunnery and methods of propulsion, the Admiralty realized that it was training men to do complex jobs and then losing them at the height of their usefulness. So by the time of *Warrior*'s first commission, men – volunteers, all of them – were signed on at 18 for ten years' service, given formal training for the job and paid regularly each month. Compare *Warrior*'s white-painted spacious lower decks with the cramped gloom of HMS *Victory*. One senses that although the pattern of a sailor's life was similar to that at the time of Trafalgar, there had been a great improvement in conditions reflecting Jolly Jack's change in status.

Late in the 1850s relations with France, never very cordial, deteriorated. In 1858 a new French fleet was commenced. The first ship was *La Gloire*, a wood-framed frigate clad in iron and the most advanced warship of its day. And further truly iron-hulled ships were planned, when industrial capacity permitted. After a royal visit to Cherbourg, Prince Albert was fuming. 'The war preparations of the French are immense,' he said, 'ours despicable. Our ministers use fine phrases but they do nothing. My blood boils within me!'

Many others shared his view and a vigorous campaign was mounted demanding that the Admiralty restore Britain's naval prestige. Their Lordships' timid first response was to suggest following the French in building an ironclad. By good fortune the new First Lord, Sir John Pakington, decided on a much bolder scheme, destined to snuff out the French threat at a stroke – the building of the world's first iron-hulled battleship.

Warrior was the brainchild of the Controller of the Navy, Admiral Baldwin Walker, and was designed by the Navy's Chief Constructor, Isaac Watts. The concept of these two men was one of an iron-framed ship with unbeatable speed, unmatched firepower and impenetrable protection. From this basic vision of a warship supreme leads a fascinating trail of knock-on design effects, culminating in the *Warrior* as we see her today.

To achieve the necessary speed in all conditions, steam power was obligatory. But with inefficient low-pressure boilers, a full load of 850 tons of coal would allow only essential manoeuvres to be carried out under steam alone. Thus sails were needed for everyday use – 48,400 square feet of them (4580m²). A maximum number of 30 men could sit on the yard arm, so the size of the biggest sail, the main topsail, was governed by what these 30 men could handle in a gale. The rest of the sails were graded accordingly.

When the ship was under sail only, the propeller, if left in the water, would create drag. Also the funnels would get in the way of the sails. So *Warrior* was equipped with a propeller that could be disengaged and lifted out of the water, and telescopic funnels that could be lowered by hand-crank.

The firepower of most wooden ships came from ranks of 32-pounder guns on several decks, but the design of these old vessels was at the limits of stability. To achieve the superior firepower of his concept, Watts's revolutionary answer was to use 68-pounders (and bigger) on one long deck – making *Warrior* technically a frigate, but at 120 feet (37m) longer than any previous warship ever built.

But these guns had to be protected

against weapons of similar destructive power. Watts surrounded them by an armoured box or 'citadel' with sealed bulkheads at each end. The box was built of 4 1/2 inch (11cm) wrought iron plate, bolted to 18 inches (46cm) of solid teak, mounted on the 5/8 inch (1.6cm) thick plating of the ship's hull. This in turn was mounted on the ship's frame, with an internal finish of pine. In tests, the most powerful guns of the day proved unable to pierce this armour, even at point-blank range! The bow and stern were to be unarmoured, but incorporating the recently developed idea of watertight compartments.

The pace of French naval expansion left no time to lose. As the Royal Dockyards were not equipped to build iron

BELOW:
The interior of the Thames Ironworks & Shipbuilding Company at Blackwall. 'The air was dense with the smoke of the forges and filled with the deafening cacophony of steam hammers forging the wrought iron plates.' Several forges are visible and, centre, one of seven giant Nasmyth steam hammers. Thames Ironworks was the biggest shipyard on the river, with considerable experience both of building iron ships and of working for the Navy.

ships, in May 1859 the keel of the new warship was laid at the Thames Ironworks, Blackwall, London. Downstream, at Penns of Greenwich, the engines and boilers began to take shape. That autumn, the ship received the name *Warrior,* inherited from a venerable ship-of-the-line recently broken up. By spring of the next year, 900 men were swarming over the huge vessel as it rose above the neighbouring rooftops. The aim was to launch *Warrior* in the summer of 1860, but because of the revolutionary

WARRIOR'S SPECIFICATIONS	
Overall length:	420 feet (128m)
Length inside:	380 feet (116m)
Beam (Width):	58 feet (18m)
Completed weight:	9,210 tons
Draught:	26 feet (8m)
Normal maximum speed:	13 knots under sail
	14.5 knots in steam
Main armament:	26 muzzle-loading 68-pdrs (31kg)
	10 breech-loading 110-pdrs (50kg)
Cost, incl. guns and coal:	£390,000

LEFT:
Warrior's massive hull rises above the rooftops at the Thames Iron-works, Blackwall, in the autumn of 1859. Armoured plates 15 feet by 3 feet (5m x 3m), weighing 4 tons each, are being bolted to a backing of East India teak. The 4 1/2" (11cm) thick plates were tongued and grooved and made from hammered scrap and puddle iron.

nature of the design and Admiralty indecision, particularly about what guns should be fitted, delays and huge cost over-runs occurred. Reaction in the newspapers swung between flag-waving patriotism and morbid doubt as to whether *War-rior* would ever touch the water.

But on 29 December 1860, *Warrior* was launched by First Lord Sir John Pakington and towed downstream to be fitted out in the Victoria Dock. By 1 August 1861, only 12 months behind *La Gloire*, *Warrior* was ready for her first commission, the largest, fastest and most powerful warship in the world.

ABOVE:
A diagram to show how the design of Warrior *was based on the concept of an armoured box or 'citadel' to protect guns and essential machinery.*

'*A black vicious ugly customer as ever I saw, whale-like in size, and with as terrible a row of incisor teeth as ever closed on a French frigate*'

CHARLES DICKENS

RIGHT:
Warrior *at Portsmouth, in 1874 for her second major refit. The engines were modified, the boilers replaced and upper deck retimbered. A 48-foot poop deck was added as admirals' accommodation and the bowsprit extended to counterbalance this.*

BELOW:
Warrior *at Plymouth in 1862 or 1863. The picture can be dated from three features: the charthouse between the funnels, new heads (just visible on the side below the funnels) both added in 1862, and the red ensign to indicate that* Warrior *was in the Channel Squadron. (From 1864, all warships flew the white ensign.) Two anchors can be seen 'catted' up at the side, as one is today.*

Unquestionably, *Warrior* ruled the seas, a living embodiment of Britain's pride in her industrial, territorial and military superiority. She never fired a shot in anger, simply because she was too powerful for any other ship even to think of challenging her. For the next three years, her main role was to lead the Channel Squadron in patrolling home waters, from northern Europe to the Eastern Atlantic. *Warrior*'s logbook reveals that, as the undisputed showpiece of the Fleet, she often escorted royalty to European cities and flew the flag in courtesy visits to home and foreign ports.

Particularly in *Warrior*'s first year of commission, Captain Cochrane's crew carried out rigorous sail, gunnery and seamanship drills to give them the feel of this revolutionary vessel and to weld them into an efficient fighting team. After an unsettled few months and two floggings, punishments decreased and a fiercely competitive spirit blossomed. The crew took particular pride in their sail evolutions – hundreds of men, swarming barefoot up the ratlines or heaving at the ropes, except for the bark-

ing of orders, in total silence. On her cruises with the squadron, endless navigation and gunnery exercises were carried out with the fleet to plan tactics.

In her career as a first-line vessel, *Warrior* in general acquitted herself well.

ABOVE:
Warrior *at full speed using steam and sail; an illustration by J.E.Wigston. The fore-course and main course sails are furled for steaming.*

WARRIOR'S CREW

42	officers
3	warrant officers
455	seamen and boys
3	Royal Marine officers
6	Royal Marine NCOs
118	Royal Marine artillerymen
2	chief engineers
10	engineers
66	stokers and trimmers

Total complement 705 men

in the ship, the steering mechanism owed more to the technology of Nelson's era, being a simple manual system of ropes and pulleys from the helm to the rudder yoke. This primitive arrangement made a ship of some 9000 tons, when she had way on, difficult to handle and very unresponsive to commands. Twice in *Warrior*'s career poor manoeuvrability resulted in accidents – on one occasion she left her figurehead on the quarterdeck of the *Royal Oak* as a much-prized souvenir.

Excitements like this were few and far between. *Warrior*'s success as a deterrent contributed to the reduction of a French invasion threat and these were quiet times for the Home Fleet. Within a year of her first commission, events were taking place on the other side of the Atlantic which were destined to make *Warrior*'s rule as 'Monarch of the Seas' very short-lived indeed.

Her fine lines meant that under sail she was one of the fastest ironclads, while under steam she consistently outperformed sister ship *Black Prince* in trials. In one respect, though, *Warrior*'s performance was not at all satisfactory. In spite of all the new advances embodied

BELOW:
In 1904 Warrior became Vernon III, *part of the HMS* Vernon *torpedo school in Portchester Creek. Her original machinery had long gone, and she was now equipped with a single funnel, boilers, generators, lathes and other machinery as well as offices, classrooms, a chapel and, on the upper deck, a gymnasium.*

The rapid evolution of warship design in the 1860s meant that in a few short years the previously mighty *Warrior* was overtaken by more advanced vessels. Just a year after *Warrior* entered service, the success of a grotesque ironclad, the *Monitor*, fighting in the Civil War on the other side of the Atlantic, was to have a dramatic effect on the thinking of naval architects. *Monitor* was short, sailless and very manoeuvrable, with all guns concentrated in an armoured turret on the upper deck. It wasn't long (1866) before the Royal Navy had ordered its first ocean-going turret ship, HMS *Captain*, although this ship still relied on auxiliary sails.

an admiral. *Warrior's* new naval and coastguard duties meant that most of the time she was in port on the south coast, emerging only five times a year to fire off her ammunition allowance or to take part in a summer cruise of reserve ships. Sadly, the former 'Monarch of the Seas' was now a 'gobby ship', a soft option for older sailors and something of an object of derision.

By 1883, even this option had run out. *Warrior* had been superseded by newer, better armed and protected ships. On 14 May she entered Portsmouth for the last time under her own power. In her 22 years of service, six of them in full commission and eight as a first-line

By the early 1870s, steam engines had improved to the point where masts and yards could be abandoned. Warships of all shapes, sizes and manner of construction followed, until *Dreadnought* of 1906 eclipsed them all.

1871, the year that introduced HMS *Devastation*, the first British ocean-going, mastless battleship, also saw the end of *Warrior's* career as a first-line warship. Ten years of service during a time of rapid change had made her obsolescent. After a last cruise with the combined fleet, she returned to Portsmouth. For the next 3¹⁄₂ years she underwent her second major refit, with the installation of improved boilers, steam power for the forward capstan and a new poop deck to accommodate

reserve, Warrior had sailed some 90,000 sea miles without ever seeing an enemy ship or firing a shot in anger.

Her engines, boilers and guns were stripped out and for several years she languished in 'Rotten Row', the tidal stream of Fareham Creek. There was occasional talk of refitting her as a cruiser, but the world's seas remained peaceful and *Warrior* was progressively forgotten. By the turn of the century, she was a mastless hulk. Her fine figurehead, however, graced the gates of the dockyard, perhaps placed there by command of Admiral Sir John Fisher, Controller of the Navy, who had served in *Warrior* as a gunnery officer in 1863–64.

In 1902, *Warrior* took on a new lease

of life as she was fitted out to become mother ship to the Portsmouth flotilla of small torpedo boats. But this role was only a brief one, for in 1904 she was converted to become part of HMS *Vernon*, the Royal Navy's floating torpedo school which was moored in Portchester Creek.

In 1923 *Vernon* moved ashore, having outgrown its sea-borne accommodation, and once more *Warrior* was paid off. But again she survived at a time when sister ship *Black Prince* and many others went to the scrapyard. She was offered for sale – but there were no takers. Finally, because the hull was still in excellent condition, *Warrior* was converted and in 1929 towed to Milford Haven for use as a floating oil jetty at Pembroke Dock. She performed this undignified task for the next 50 years, during which time all her hitherto surviving contemporaries went to the breakers. When in 1960, HMS *Vanguard* submitted to the cutting torch, *Warrior* remained as Britain's last surviving battleship – a fact not lost upon several influential people.

ABOVE:
A melancholy sight. Her days as Vernon III over, and with no buyers because the price of scrap was so low, Warrior *is towed across Portsmouth Harbour in 1923 to languish once more as a hulk in 'Rotten Row'.*

LEFT:
In 1929, because of her basically sound condition, Warrior *was converted as a fuelling hulk to serve at Llannion Cove, Pembroke Dock in Milford Haven, Wales. For 50 years ships loaded and unloaded oil alongside, and she was home to several generations of shipkeepers and their families. In 1942 she became* Oil Fuelling Hulk C77 *to make way for the new HMS* Warrior, *a Canadian aircraft carrier.*

BELOW RIGHT:
Warrior at Hartlepool, 1979. The first challenge that faced her restorers was to remove 80 tons of accumulated rubbish, then strip off 200 tons of concrete from her rotted upper deck. 140 skilled craftsmen helped restore Warrior. *Before restoration, every relevant item within the ship was carefully examined, photographed and catalogued.*

BELOW:
A stern view in Hartlepool Dock. The propellor well is just visible above the water level. Because of this and the steering yoke above the rudder, a traditional stern gallery was not possible – the appearance of one is purely for decoration.

It was in 1967 that people first talked of restoring *Warrior*. Prominent in this campaign was John Smith, at that time MP for the City of Westminster, who had formed the Manifold Trust five years earlier to restore threatened items of our national heritage. Smith's drive and persistence led to a committee, chaired by the Duke of Edinburgh, meeting in 1968 to discuss *Warrior*'s future. From this emerged the Maritime Trust, formed to raise money for the preservation of our naval heritage. As for *Warrior*, several ideas were mooted but nothing firm was decided for, after all, she was still in use in Milford Haven.

In 1976 word came that the fuel depot was to close in two years' time and that *Warrior* would no longer be needed. John Smith agreed that the Manifold Trust would underwrite the costs of restoration, estimated at between £4 million and £8 million, and the ship was handed over to the Maritime Trust. The work was to take place at the north-eastern port of Hartlepool, where she was towed in autumn 1979.

Although *Warrior*'s hull was sound, the rest of the ship was in a terrible state. The task – part restoration, part rebuilding – was enormous and would need vast resources, not only of money but also of skill, patience and endurance. In addition there was an immense amount of research to be done all over the country to unearth the details necessary for reconstruction. Everything was photographed and all items painstakingly logged and stored. Gradually a complete picture emerged of what *Warrior* had been like at the time of her first commission. Ship's plans had identified the main features of the structure; a less likely but invaluable source was the journal of one of *Warrior*'s midshipmen, 14-year-old Henry Murray, who had drawn detailed plans of the ship's decks and where everything was.

A workforce of 140 moved into the ship and, after clearing away over 80 tons of debris, started the dark, damp and difficult task of restoration. In 1981 *Warrior* was given a new upper deck of Victorian timber from the floors of a demolished Bradford warehouse. (Some of the main deck and most of the lower deck timber is original.) In 1984 she received her masts, and in 1985 a re-created figurehead (the original had survived until 1963). In the bowels of the ship, several years were spent in stripping old paint (as many as 120 layers of it), repainting and re-creating the boiler and engine rooms as they would have looked. By amazing good luck, guns were found of the type first fitted in *Warrior*, and fibreglass replicas made. As today's visitor can see, no detail was overlooked – from ropes and hammocks to the mess plates and the captain's pictures – everything chosen and placed with loving care.

Now *Warrior* was fully rigged and ready, a worthy tribute to all those involved in her restoration. Portsmouth was to be her base once more, and on 16 June 1987, 58 years after leaving as a forgotten and decaying hulk, amid memorable scenes, she came home.

ABOVE:
Work being carried out on the brass slide and pivot carriage for one of the upper-deck Armstrong 110-pdr guns.

LEFT:
Warrior's figurehead was carved in the Isle of Wight. The original was made in Portsmouth at a cost of £60, only to be left on the deck of HMS Royal Oak *in an 1868 collision. After* Warrior *ceased active service, its successor graced the main gates of Portsmouth dockyard and later HMS* Warrior *(Northwood) until as recently as 1963, when it succumbed to a harsh winter.*

LEFT:
The newly restored HMS Warrior 1860, *accompanied by a flotilla of wellwishers, passes Southsea front on 16 June 1987, en route to her £1¹/2 million permanent berth at the Royal Naval Dockyard, Portsmouth.*

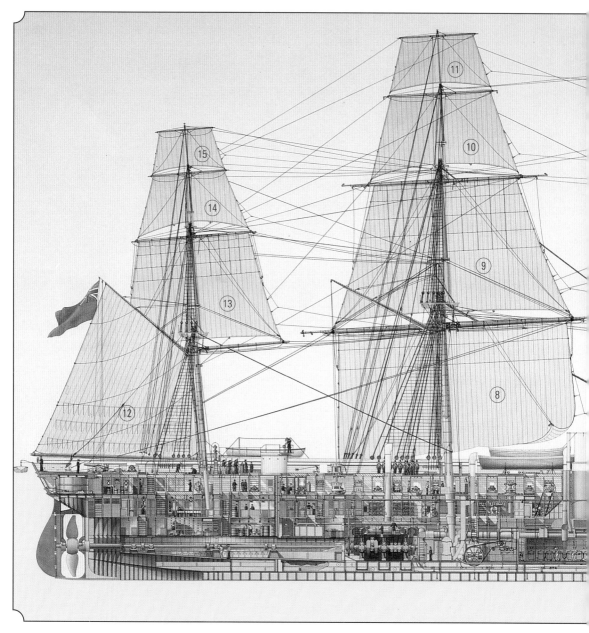

ABOVE:
A cutaway drawing of Warrior *as she was in 1861, drawn by Stephen Ortega of Bournemouth and Poole College of Art and Design.*

The ship at sea under sail, with its funnels cranked down to their lower position. A certain amount of artistic licence is involved, however, as the propeller is seen in position for steaming, when in reality it would have been raised.

We can see officers standing on the forward and after bridges, quartermaster and helmsmen at the steering wheels and officers and men attending to the normal duties of the day on the mess decks, in the engine room and stokeholds. Certain of *Warrior*'s original features are depicted which are not part of the restored ship: the propeller shaft; the forward magazine; the auxiliary boiler room engine; various storerooms; the sick bay on the lower deck, forward of the mainmast.

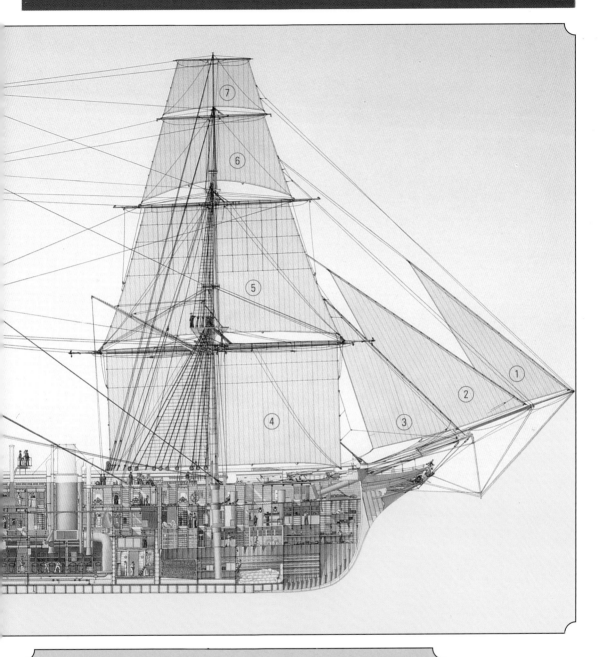

KEY TO WORKING CANVAS

1	Flying jib	8	Main course
2	Jib	9	Main topsail
3	Staysail	10	Main top gallant
4	Fore course	11	Main royal
5	Fore topsail	12	Spanker
6	Fore topgallant	13	Mizzen topsail
7	Fore royal	14	Mizzen topgallant
		15	Mizzen royal

This is a spacious working deck, where the ship was (usually) steered, where hundreds of sailors manhandled the yards, sails and rigging, where boats were hoisted and lowered and where drills were carried out. There were even sheep kept in pens up here for fresh meat on a long voyage, with chickens and ducks in the boats!

As in HMS *Victory*, up amongst the masts and yards are the fighting tops, platforms where Marine riflemen took aim during close-in fighting. All around the deck are high bulwarks to defend against boarders. It is interesting that, in fitting *Warrior* with features such as fighting tops and bulwarks, the designers failed to anticipate that the power of *Warrior*'s guns would make close fighting, of the sort that took place at Trafalgar, a thing of the past.

There are two bridges on the deck, much more like the real bridges which gave rise to the term than the protected navigation rooms of modern ships. The Captain directed fighting from the after bridge or from the armoured conning tower, while the ship was navigated from the forward bridge. Commands were relayed by a system of voicepipes and manual telegraphs. There are eight compasses – the steering compasses being fitted in pairs for easy visibility. In *Warrior*'s heyday, the compass was still the 'instrument pregnant with mischief' that sailors of old knew and cursed. The

LEFT:
The helm. It took over three turns of the wheel to go from midship to hard astarboard or vice versa. It was not unusual to have 16 men at the wheel, wrestling to keep the ship in check. The central dial is the rudder indicator, and on either side two of the Evans pillar binnacles.

BELOW:
At the stern, amongst the brass pivots and racers for the 110-pdr gun, a circle cut in the deck marks the propeller well. Sheer-legs were erected and the 'ruddy old twiddler' – 24 tons of propeller plus an 8-ton banjo frame – was raised for periods of sail-only sailing. It took about 600 men to do it. The drawing is by Gary Cook.

reason for this was the deviation, up to 30°, caused by the ship's iron hull. This unfortunate trait was accentuated when the ship rolled in heavy seas. All that Their Lordships could do was to conduct rolling tests in harbour, measure the degree of deviation and compensate for it accordingly.

At the bow, the huge bowsprit soars outwards above the figurehead. This was shortened very early in *Warrior*'s life when the ship was found to be bow-heavy. Beyond the bulwark here and just visible are the heads (toilets) – two lines of five holes directly above the water. *Warrior*'s clipper-style bow meant a great deal of water breaking over the bow – not too pleasant for the sitting tenants – so compartments at the side of the ship were soon added. The diamond-shaped metal objects at the bow are marker buoys which were always used in letting go an anchor in case it was fouled or, in emergency, had to be slipped and left for later recovery.

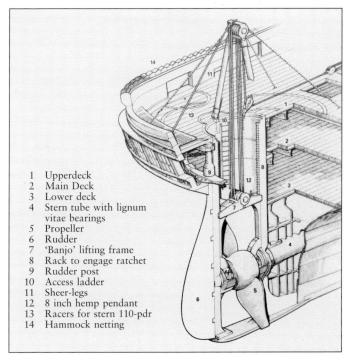

1 Upperdeck
2 Main Deck
3 Lower deck
4 Stern tube with lignum vitae bearings
5 Propeller
6 Rudder
7 'Banjo' lifting frame
8 Rack to engage ratchet
9 Rudder post
10 Access ladder
11 Sheer-legs
12 8 inch hemp pendant
13 Racers for stern 110-pdr
14 Hammock netting

The gun or main deck represents the heart of *Warrior*, for the ship's firepower was the main reason for her existence, and it was here that nearly all the crew spent most of their time – eating and sleeping in 'messes' between the guns. There were 28 messes in the citadel, with 18 men or so in each. Each mess had a table which could be triced up out of the way as necessary. Hammocks were slung on hooks between the deck beams, amongst the rammers and sponges used in firing the guns.

On the gun deck, the main part of *Warrior*'s massive firepower was twenty six 68-pounder muzzle-loading guns. These had an effective range of 2,500 yards (2,300m) and fired mainly round projectiles – iron shot (black), stone shot (red) or shells filled with various lethal ingredients. These guns were reliable and effective, a larger version of a tried and trusted design evolved over many years. Also installed were eight Armstrong 110-pounder breech-loading guns, with a range of over 4500 yards (4150m). These were so new that the decision to fit them was taken only while *Warrior* was being built. They had rifled barrels

for greater accuracy, and fired cone-headed, lead-coated shot or shell (the lead 'bit' into the rifling). Being innovatory, these guns were on trial, but they proved too prone to accidents, having a dangerous tendency to overheat and blow out the breech block. In 1863 most of the Armstrong guns were sold off to Confederate forces in America.

Warrior's guns were never fired in anger, but at least once a week gun crews were thoroughly drilled, and there was intense competition for the quarterly and annual prizes for best gun crew. It is nearly impossible to describe the unbearable heat, smoke, noise and frenzied (but ordered) activity that went into the firing of the guns. The order 'Clear for action!' is shouted. Tables are triced up and the deck sanded for better grip. Up to now the 68-pounders have been angled upwards and tied to the bulkhead out of the way. Now, on the command 'Cast loose!' the guns come down, the gunports are heaved open, eyebolts are screwed in to the deckplate and the guns and their tackle roped to them. In the meantime, a leather container of powder, enough for three rounds, has been handed up from the magazine below through the scuttles in the deck near the after and forward

bulkheads. Ready for loading, a gun is hauled 6 feet (2m) back from the gunport and levered with poles to the correct angle, using the marks on the deckhead above. Two men carry a round shot to the gun on a special flower-shaped rope 'garland'. On 'Load the guns!', the bag of gunpowder is pushed down the muzzle, followed by a rope grommet, the shot and another grommet – all rammed in with a rod. The gun is hauled forward, and the gun

captain 'spikes' the gun, inserting a percussion tube including a cap which acted as a detonator. On the command 'Fire', the captains pull their firing lanyards and 19 guns speak simultaneously in a deafening roar, hurtling backwards on their trucks. Amid the ensuing bedlam of smoke and noise, the guns are sponged out, barrels cooled with wet flails, powder containers dropped to the magazine for refilling, and the frantic sequence begins again.

Beyond the forward bulkhead is the manger, so named because cows were kept here for fresh meat during a long voyage. The petty officers messed here, aloof from the rest of the men. Four guns are missing from the forward ports, moved aft in 1862 to make *Warrior* less bow-heavy.

The Royal Marines in the ship messed at the aft end of the citadel. Beyond the after bulkhead is the afterguard, which was the officers' recreational area. Here Marine sentries were always on duty, a throwback to the days when sailors were pressed into service and there was always the possibility of mutiny. (By all accounts, though, *Warrior* was a well-run, happy ship during her first-line career.)

ABOVE:
The gun deck. Here 600 men spent most of their time. The guns in the picture are 68-pdr muzzle loaders, traditional but reliable.

LEFT CENTRE:
The afterguard. The officers used this area for recreation. A Marine sentry was always on duty here. On the left, a crocus of Navy Colt revolvers for officers' use.

LEFT INSET:
Warrior *had 350 Enfield muzzle-loading rifles – seamen's with cutlass, bayonet and brown sling, Marines' with serrated bayonet and a white sling. The buckets are in case of fire.*

'Six days shalt thou labour – and on the seventh work harder than ever.'

OLD NAVAL SAYING

O f *Warrior's* 700 crew, 600 men were needed purely as muscle power – although gun crews and yardmen needed skill as well. Seamen were needed to man the guns, hoist sails, turn capstans, haul on ropes, hoist and lower boats, pull on oars and crank the Downton pumps which moved water from one part of the ship to another. Stokers and trimmers had the hardest physical work down below in the boiler room (see page 26).

Besides sail evolutions, the most regular job involving large-scale teamwork was raising the anchor. *Warrior's* four 5.6-ton anchors at bow and stern were the heaviest in maritime history to be operated manually. These were hauled up one at a time by linked capstans, the chain going into cable lockers (positioned amidships to keep the ship's balance). Each capstan accommodated 100 men

plus several more on the swifter, a rope which linked the ends of the capstan bars. Once out of the water, the anchors were 'catted' up as we see one today.

Coaling the ship took place every few weeks as necessary, given suitable port facilities. It involved the *whole* crew in laborious, dirty and sometimes hazardous work. The gun deck was cleared, with tables up, guns back and ports open. Seamen and marines filled 2cwt (100kg) wicker panniers aboard the collier berthed alongside. These were hauled through the gunports, lifted over the deck and emptied through six chutes to stokers waiting in the bunkers below.

A Typical Day's Timetable at Sea	
Coil up ropes	03.30
Scrub decks	04.00
Re-set sails	05.45
Stow hammocks	06.00
Breakfast	06.30
Cleaning tasks	07.15
Prayers	09.00
Drills	09.30
Dinner	12.00
Roll call	13.25
Drills	13.30
Supper	16.15
Quarters	17.00
Stand by hammocks	19.30
Rounds	20.30

It took two days for the full capacity of 850 tons to be loaded. The ship's 16-piece band would play stirring tunes to help the coaling along. By the end of the operation, dust from the dry coal (and it had to be very dry) would have so blackened the gun deck that cleaning ship afterwards often took a week in itself.

On Sundays, after Captain's rounds and divisions (the men lining up in their work sections – gunners, marines, stokers, etc.), attendance at a church service (usually on the main deck) was compulsory. After Sunday dinner a man's time was his own; he also had some recreation time on weekdays during the dog watches (4–8pm). Concerts were popular, with everybody including the officers expected to take a turn now and then.

An 1863 visitor to the main deck during recreation time describes men asleep in their hammocks, others sitting at the mess table eating their 'levener' (elevenses in our terms), playing cards, reading and writing letters. Somebody was singing, others were embroidering and quilting.

The seaman of 1860 was trained properly, paid monthly and had chosen to sign up for at least ten years. A reflection of the fact that conditions were so much better than they were just a few years before, the typical sailor tended to be a quiet family man, very different in outlook from the not-so-jolly jack of Nelson's day.

LEFT:
The infamous cat o'nine tails which could reduce a man's back to raw meat with ten lashes. It was kept in this bag – hence the saying 'to let the cat out of the bag'. On Warrior's first commission, two men were flogged (48 and 36 lashes) for theft, but use of the cat was much more restricted than in Nelson's day. The cane was used on those under 18.

BOTTOM LEFT:
The cells were used for men who had committed serious crimes; absence over leave, disobedience, sleeping on watch, etc. Picking oakum was a common punishment here – pulling old rope to pieces for caulking the deck etc. In 1860, this cell would have been smaller, for there was then a passage behind. Serious wrongdoing was much less of a problem in the Navy of 1860 than in earlier times. Most punishments involved men being put on the 'black list' which entailed a very harsh regime of extra duties.

BOTTOM RIGHT:
A ditty box for the sailor's day-to-day possessions. The knife was used for eating as well as cutting ropes, canvas, etc. The sharp tool is a pricker for making holes in canvas, the 'mushroom' for darning. The open wallet is a sailor's 'housewife' for all his sewing equipment. The bone is for ornamental whittling.

Because so much of a Victorian sailor's life was spent doing heavy physical work, food was plentiful in quantity, if variable in quality. As there was no refrigeration, fresh food ran out soon after the ship put to sea. After that it was 'hard tack' – salt meat, dried vegetables and ship's biscuit. Breakfast usually consisted of kye (cocoa) and biscuit or bread, with preserves or cheese. The main meal of the day, taken at noon, would usually be soup or porridge, boiled meat and cabbage or similar vegetable, spotted dick (a heavy suet pudding with raisins), followed by tea or kye. The evening meal would usually be a cold version of the midday meal. Moves were afoot to improve the men's diet, but the Victorian sailor was strangely attached to

The coal-fired galley was manned by seamen who because of age or disablement were unfit for more vigorous duties. The nearest that these old salts came to a knowledge of cookery was knowing how to boil water in the large tanks on the galley stove. The mess cook also had to clear the table and organize the wooden kits, kegs and kettles that held supplies of different sorts.

Stewards organized the preparation of meals for the Captain and officers. It is debatable whether their food was cooked separately and whether it differed in standard from that eaten by the men, but it would certainly have been supplemented by officers' private purchases, particularly when in port or at buoy offshore.

Water was limited. A whole mess of 18 or more men would only get two tubfuls of cold water twice a week to wash in. Only the men in the boiler room washed or bathed daily. Some 120 tons of fresh water was carried in tanks located fore and aft over the magazines and there was a small still for distilling sea water.

Of more interest to the average seaman was his daily ration of grog, a mixture of 2 parts water to 1 part rum. Approximately half a pint of this was ceremonially issued at 12.30 and carried back from the rum room in a metal container by the mess cook.

Spitting was much more usual and accepted than it is today. Tuberculosis was a very common disease in damp, cold ships (and iron vessels were infa-

what would seem to us stodgy and unattractive fare.

Every seaman took turns to do a week's duty as mess cook, having to: collect his mess's ration of food from the issuing room on the lower deck; chop up the (usually) salted meat, pickled cabbage, etc. and put them in separate string bags (which had numbered copper tags to identify them); make a pudding from flour, raisins, suet and sugar, and bag it in muslin; take the bags to and from the galley on the gun deck.

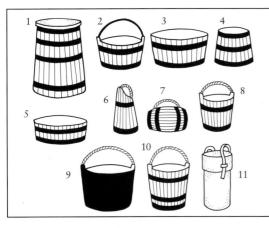

MESS CONTAINERS

1   Bread bin
2   Hot water bucket
3   Tub for collecting food issues
4   Keg for grog
5   Spit kid
6   Can for water
7   Barricoe for vinegar
8   Night bucket
9   Swab bucket
10 Fire bucket
11 Cartridge case for powder

BELOW:
Three of Warrior's modern-day quarter-masters on the upper deck in the authentic uniform of 1860. The upper deck planking was entirely renewed during the restoration, having rotted for 50 years beneath six inches of concrete. (Victorian timber from a Bradford warehouse was used.)

mously cold); as there were no drugs to treat it then, spitting was the only way of trying to clear congested lungs. Also many sailors bought tobacco each month which they would either smoke in pipes, or chew before spitting out. Neighbouring messes on the main deck shared a wooden spit kit for this purpose. Officers tended to smoke pipes or cigars on the upper deck in the evening.

The introduction of a sailor's uniform in 1859 was yet another sign that things had changed in the Navy. Dress varied according to the job, the day of the week and the time of day. Very dark blue jumpers and white trousers formed the most normal outfit, but white dress was worn for drills. Stokers wore white duck suits all the time. On Sundays, hats were always worn (except in wet weather!) – black in winter, white in summer. Clothes were issued monthly from the Paymaster's slops (the Navy word for clothing) and the cost deducted from a seaman's pay.

Of critical importance to *Warrior's* well-being was the Paymaster who, as the ship's accountant, controlled victualling, clothes and pay from his office on the lower deck.

Pay parade was a formal affair which took place monthly. Offwatch seamen reported to the pay office on the main deck. At the command, a seaman would remove his hat and his money would be placed in it. Levels of pay ranged from that of the Captain, who was paid £1 per day to that of a Boy 2nd Class who got 6d (2½p) per day.

A SAILOR'S FOOD AND DRINK RATION

Daily:	1¼ lbs (570g)	bread or biscuit
	1 lb (450g)	fresh meat (if available)
	1 lb (450g)	fresh vegetables (if available)
	1 lb (450g)	salt pork + ⅓ pint (190ml) peas
or	1 lb (450g)	salt beef
	9 oz (250g)	flour
	¾ oz (20g)	suet
	1½ oz (40g)	currants or raisins
	2 oz (56g)	sugar
	1 oz (28g)	chocolate (for cocoa)
	¼ oz (7g)	tea
	⅛ pint (70ml)	spirits (normally rum)
Weekly:	¼ pint (140ml)	oatmeal
	¼ pint (140ml)	vinegar
	½ oz (14g)	mustard
	¼ oz (7g)	pepper

BELOW RIGHT:
The wardroom. The officers had their own wardroom stewards to serve them. The dining table would become an operating table in time of battle. Warrior's wardroom enjoyed the distinction that at times sunlight could penetrate from above.

BELOW:
The Captain's cabin. In ships of the period, these were furnished very much like Victorian drawing rooms. The Captain had his own heads and walking space in the after area near the propeller well and steering yoke. Note the auxiliary steering ropes passing through at deckhead level. Warrior's first Captain, the Hon. Arthur Cochrane, was thought by many to be the most brilliant and daring commander of the 19th century. Not only was he a good seaman and a natural leader, but he had inherited a natural resource and a flair for technical matters.

Warrior had a very strict hierarchy of command – which survives to a great extent in today's Navy. The Captain, responsible to the Admiralty for everything and everybody on board, was the absolute ruler of his ship, with the power to make or break the careers of his men. He had spacious quarters aft on the main deck, with a sleeping and day cabin and his own heads. Unlike those in *Victory* the Captain's quarters were not in the traditional aftermost part, because of the space taken up by the rudder yoke and propeller well. The Captain's personal steward worked from a pantry nearby.

The Commander, the ship's No.2, was responsible for the ship's fighting ability and its general appearance, besides being president of the wardroom mess. The only other officer on the main deck was the Master, often an older man. He was the expert on sailing and

navigation and would con the ship in action. The title of 'Master' was a throwback to the days when merchant ships and their masters were commandeered for naval use, to work under a Navy captain.

The wardroom, on the lower deck, was the mess for the other officers, with 14 cabins off a central dining and relaxation area. (In former times, the wardroom had been a store for treasure from captured vessels; officers had moved in to protect their share!) The Captain could only enter the wardroom by invitation – some indication of the often lonely job he had.

Some of the younger wardroom members would have been graduates of the new officer training school on *Illus-*

trious or later *Britannia*. The ship's chaplain usually doubled as schoolmaster, not just for the men but also for mates (sub-lieutenants) and snotties (midshipmen).

These youngsters, 20 or 30 of them, lived a less formal life in their lower deck mess, the gunroom (historically, the chief gunner had been in charge of the snotties). They slept in hammocks wherever they could find space. One midshipman, Henry Murray, aged 14 when he joined

Warrior in 1861, drew in his journal plans of the ship's decks, showing all equipment in its position. These are still in existence, and proved immensely useful in the ship's restoration. Elsewhere on the lower deck were messes and cabins for the lower-ranking engineers, the boatswain, the gunner, the carpenter and the chief petty officers.

ABOVE:
The Captain's night cabin. Although the cot here is like Nelson's in HMS Victory, *it is by no means certain what Captain Cochrane slept on, for such was his authority that he could have chosen even a four poster bed had he so wished!*

LEFT ABOVE:
An officer's cabin. His sea chest would have been stored in the hold, but he has his recreational equipment with him. Trousers were not hung up but pressed beneath the mattress.

LEFT:
Warrior's officers on deck in c. 1869, a period of the ship's working life when discipline was strict and morale very high. It was in this year that Warrior *played her part in towing a new floating dock 4,000 miles (6,400km) to Bermuda.*

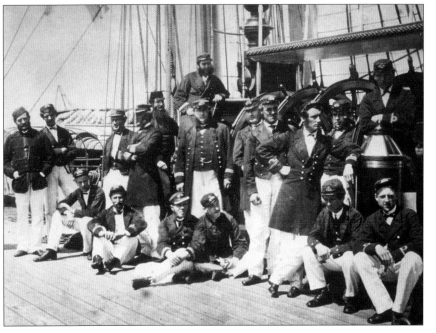

BELOW:
The boiler room or stokehold. During trials in 1861 the temperature reached 129°F (54°C) in here. At any one time two of the ten boilers would be out of action in rotation for descaling and repair.

BELOW CENTRE:
A cross section. Note the funnel, the extent of the teak-backed armour plating 6 feet (2m) below the water line, the racks for kitbags on the lower deck and the coal bunkers behind the boilers.

It is small wonder that *Warrior*'s stokers and trimmers were paid 50% more than able seamen, for conditions in the stokehold were truly dreadful. Down here men toiled away for hours shovelling tons of coal and ash by hand in a heat of around 110°F (43°C). The air was thick with dust and the noise indescribable.

Warrior had ten boilers, each with four furnaces. The coal was stored in eight bunkers along the outside of the engine and boiler rooms. Every ounce of the 850 tons of it had to be moved by hand, from the back to the front of the bunker, from the bunker to the furnace door, from the door several feet into the furnace. To help the trimmers (the men who shovelled coal from the bunkers), small trucks ran on rails 100 feet (30m) long from the bunkers, located behind the boilers, to the furnace doors.

Besides keeping the furnaces evenly fed with fuel, the stokers had continually to separate and remove white-hot ash and clinker from the fires, facing the heat as they did so. Ash was raked out with a 3-metre slice onto the boiler plate (floor) and doused with jets of water from a leather hose, the red-hot slice being flung into the racks above. Later the piles of ash were put into ash buckets and hoisted mechanically to the upper deck for tipping overboard down special chutes. The auxiliary engine which drove this hoist and provided some degree of ventilation was located in the space which today's visitor passes en route to the engine room.

In visiting the engine room, it should be kept in mind that the lazy, silent action of the reproduction twin-cylinder trunk engine that we see now is a far cry from the sight and sound here in *Warrior*'s heyday. Then the engine room would have been a dimly-lit cavern, filled with the 'humph-humph-grind' and the hiss of steam of the twin cylinders as they turned the shaft more than twenty times faster than today's reproduction.

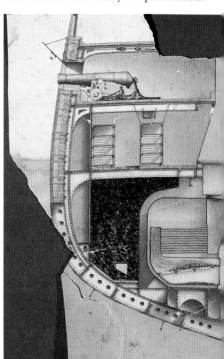

LEFT:
The horizontal trunk engine took up less space than its predecessors, and being below the water line was less vulnerable to attack. The trunk (a tube running through the cylinder) attached direct to a short rod connecting piston to crank, thus halving the normal distance involved. The reproduction engine today revolves at 2 1/2 r.p.m. The normal operating speed of the original was 56 r.p.m.

BELOW:
Heated shot was especially deadly in setting fire to enemy wooden ships. Scrap metal was heated in this cupola furnace then poured into shells which were hoisted to the gun deck for firing.

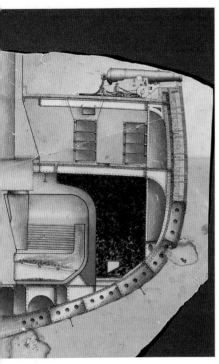

of the seamen with the spacious luxury and furnishings enjoyed by the Captain and officers. Visitors can view the working reproduction of the magnificent Penn horizontal trunk steam engine on their way from seeing the reconstructed boilers in the stokehold. Authenticity extends to the Quartermasters on board, who wear the correct naval uniforms of the period.

Warrior is the only surviving embodiment of the most revolutionary changes to take place in the long and distinguished history of the Royal Navy, spanning the era of wood and iron and of sail and steam, as well as offering a valuable insight into the technological and scientific progress of the Victorians. The contrast with nearby HMS *Victory* is a fascinating one. Because it is such a unique primary historical source, the ship is visited throughout the year by many school parties of all ages. Groups can choose either a self-guided visit (a team of very knowledgeable and accomplished *Warrior* volunteers on board is always happy to answer any questions) or pre-book a number of different activity-based programmes on offer.

ABOVE:
Warrior is an increasingly popular location for feature films, television and photoshoots.

RIGHT:
In January 1994, Warrior *was dry docked and her condition thoroughly examined by experts. As part of a major overhaul, the hull was cleaned and recoated with a protective layer of bituminous enamel paint, applied at 200°C. The masts were repainted and the rigging checked for wear and tear before* Warrior *was returned to her berth.*

HMS *Warrior* 1860 is now a permanent feature of Portsmouth's skyline. Her dominant position at the entrance to the historic Naval Base, home to the Royal Navy Museum and three of the world's most famous ships, means she is one of the city's most visible attractions. *Warrior* has proved to be enormously popular with people of all ages and nationalities, attracting an average of 200,000 visitors per year since the ship's public opening in 1987.

As they explore four decks at their leisure, visitors are given a unique glimpse of life aboard a 19th-century warship – and not just a glimpse, for there are so many things to touch! They can sit at the mess tables on the main deck, examine *Warrior*'s formidable firepower and compare the spartan existence